BATTLE CRY

BATTLE
CRY

POEMS

JENNIFER
SARA
WIDELITZ

atmosphere press

CONTENTS

Poetry is like a fine wine:
it should be sipped—
each word savored
on the tongue,
it's richness
and timeless potency
contemplated
to the last
d
r
o
p
.

Poetry is art in writing,
where each letter is a brushstroke
that paints a picture composed
of a thousand words.

But sometimes painting a rainbow
is the hardest thing
to do when all you've been
experiencing is the rain.

THIS BOOK BELONGS TO...

- The person struggling with a debilitating illness.
- The person struggling to help someone with a debilitating illness.
- The person struggling to cope with circumstances beyond one's control.
- The person struggling with life in general.
- The person who wants to scream but smiles instead.
- The person who smiles but falls asleep on tear-soaked pillows.
- The person looking for someone who also knows the salty taste of tears.
- The comforter who needs to be comforted.
- The person who can feel alone in a sold-out stadium.
- The wanderer trying to find a place in the world.
- The optimist attempting to see the beauty in their surroundings.
- The pessimist attempting to see the beauty in their surroundings.
- The dreamer who wants to make the world a better place.
- The person who is trying to love a body that is broken and tearing itself apart.
- The brave heart who is broken and asking for help.
- The brave heart who is broken and not ready to ask for help.
- The individual searching for a kindred soul.
- The kind, the sad, the lost and forgotten, the drinkers, the tinkers, and the over-thinkers.
- The one who collects books like others collect coins or stamps.
- The connoisseur who drinks in words like they are water.
- The lonely lover.
- The artist without a muse.
- The poet who hasn't found their words.

- The leader who is building up the courage to speak.
- The rebel, the warrior, the comrade-in-arms who will not surrender without a fight.
- The person who is stronger than they realize.
- The survivor of the human condition.
- You:
- _____

For my loving family:
Tracey, Sabrina, Scott, Honey Bun, and Binx.

For you:
the strongest of warriors.

BEFORE

CHILDHOOD FANTASIES

I have never desired to be
the princess—a helpless damsel,
dressed in shimmering tiaras
and gowns of pink and white—

nor have I ever preferred to be
clad in heavy armor
as an oath-sworn,
horseback-riding knight.

I have always wished, instead, to be
a timeless tale, a formidable legend
that is only spoken of
in the dark confines of night,

to have no fear of bowing
and the strength to stand my ground,
yet, when the need should arise,
to spread my wings and take flight—

to be the sometimes feared,
but always respected,
powerful dragon
known for her fearsome might.

SWING

In the dawn of childhood,
we swing on wooden planks
held by metal chains,
reaching for our dreams
that are kept safely
amongst the clouds.

DANCE LESSONS

Ballet never taught
me to twirl with grace,
and hip hop never helped
me to feel the beat.

No amount of dance lessons
filled my soul like learning
to dance to the drumming
rhythm of my own heart.

TREASURE

Treasure is not always
glittering gold and sparkling jewels
buried beneath the sand.

Treasure is often the smiles
hidden between the dusty
pages of photo albums,

their true value
not appraised
until it is too late.

SEQUINS

(for my mother)

You are like golden sequins
in evening candlelight:
some surfaces hidden from view,
while others reflect prisms
of color when regarded
at just the right angle.
Sometimes dark, sometimes light,
but always a shimmering
beauty to behold.

SHOES TO FILL

I always lived in her shadow,
believing her to be the sun
when she was only blocking its light.

I look like her,
but not nearly enough.
I stagger clumsily

as she sashays
into the room,
commanding all attention.

Her heels are too high,
and my feet are too large
to even consider trying them on.

SUNSHINE AND SAND

(for my sister)

You are an endless summer
of sunshine and sand,
longing for a winter breeze
to cool your burning heart.

TOY CARS AND DINOSAURS

I often reminisce
about the days of old,
when stories were read
under the blanket
of night, the floors
were littered with
toy cars and dinosaurs,
and our doors were adjacent
like our beating hearts.

ANCIENT

I miss the care-free days
measured by the easy smiles
that tugged at our lips.

I fear they are now beyond reach,
for the sun has set on those times,
and they are now ancient history.

BUBBLES AND BLUE SKIES

Bubbles, like dreams,
reflect glimmers of light
as they reach skyward,
and leave you with
nothing when they burst.

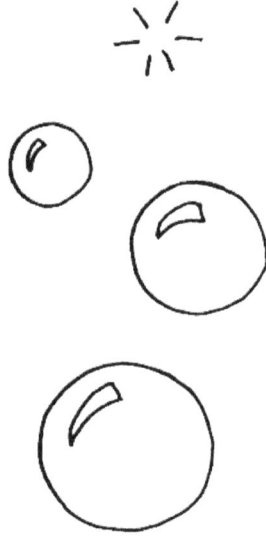

WISHBONES

Please wish and dream
and fill your soul
with hope—

keep your eye out for a four-leaf clover,
toss a coin into every well,
whisper to the brightest star—

but keep in mind
that wishbones snap
just as easily as hearts.

ROTTING APPLES

No one likes to hear about
how so much pain and misfortune
could rot even the best of us,
that wicked people are not born evil.

Yet many seem to forget that the Evil Queen
was once a hopeful young princess,
and that the Big Bad Wolf was once a pup
who howled his wishes to the moon.

DIFFERENT ENDINGS

There are some girls who read
fairytales and befriend the witch
and the wolf,
knowing their stories would have ended
differently if they had someone to listen
and a hand to hold.

CRASH

PLUCKING PETALS

She will love him,
he will love her not.

He will discover happiness,
she will not.

She will find success,
he will not.

He will be healthy,
she will not.

Life plucks the petals,
leaving us to step
on the thorns.

BUILDING ROME

I.

Nothing was built in a day,
except for a house of cards.

II.

Nothing lasting was established
within the constraints of a single day.
Not Rome, trust, health, or society.
But like a house of cards,
they can all crumble in one.

LEGEND

Sometimes,
legends do not last.

Sometimes,
all that will remain

are snippets of the whisper
that once was whole,

lost forever
on the winds of change.

CRASH [krash] :
> (v.) *to break into or fall to pieces violently and noisily; shatter.*
> (n.) *a breaking or falling to pieces with loud noise.*

but there was no noise,
no explosion of light or sound,
no moment in time to pinpoint
the instant everything changed.

This grew over time, unnoticed,

like an undetected tumor
forming silently beneath the skin
until one day it refused to be ignored,

like a whisper, so soft
it couldn't be heard
until it swelled into a roar,

like an unknown leak,
accumulating drop by drop
until it flooded the ground floor,

like adding a rock to a backpack
every few yards on a long hike
until the weight became unbearable.

COLD WAVES

Cold waves of air
lapping at my skin,
providing a little
relief to the searing
pain, and, at least,
giving me something
else to focus on,
refreshing my lungs
that were once
filled with the
stale air of the past.

ABANDONED

My body feels
like the creaking floors
of an abandoned house,

my room
the shell of a memory
I used to covet.

REFLECTIONS

The truth behind every reflection
is hidden beneath the surface,
beneath every lie and every scar
that has transformed the face
staring back at me,
the unmistakable image
I no longer recognize.

RORSCHACH TEST: INKBLOT # 3, BEFORE AND AFTER

Note: This poem can be read top to bottom, and bottom to top.

"I see trees."
Scraggly brushes
Paint a sunrise with
Soft oranges and blues of dawn
Spilling across a sleepy world like pale watercolors
Gliding across wet virginal paper,
Birds sing in welcome of a new day, a sky-bound parade.
Reflected in the placid waters, moments echo on the mirrored surface.
Birds scatter in frantic escape, sky-bound for new horizons.
Protruding from ancient waters,
Slicing across a gloomy world like sharp razorblades
Diluted blood and tinges of tears
Stain a sunset with
Gnarled fingers
"I see trees."

NO PLACE TO HIDE: I

The darkness knows me like no one else.
For in the night, there is no trick of the light,
and no way to hide the contents of my heart.

SNAPPED

One day, something inside
me snapped,
like a rubber band pulled
too tightly.

TIME DOES NOT ALWAYS SLIP AWAY

Time does not always slip away.

Sometimes he stands
before you, taunting,
waiting,

waiting for you to reach
out and take his hand.

And the worst part
is that you can't—

no matter how much you try,
no matter how much it pains you
not to do so—

you can't even lift your arm,
let alone seize time
while you still have him.

Sometimes all you can do is stare—
you don't take your eyes
off Time,

because you know that once you blink,
he will have vanished.

So you and Time remain still,
motionless,
gazes unwavering.

Unfortunately,
Time has the advantage—
Time needs no rest.

But you succumb to the sleepy
influence of the night,
and when you awake,
Time has gone—

flown away on the wings of dreams
and the tails of stars.

And yet, you awake
unmoved.

Nothing changed
except for time.

CASSANDRA'S CRY

To know something is desperately wrong
that others do not believe
is beyond upsetting—frustrating,
distressing, nauseating,
like trying to scream
but no sound escapes—
especially when they start to think
that the issue is *you*.
I now understand how Cassandra
must have felt.

TEST RESULTS

You want the tests
to come back negative—
you pray that they do,

yet a small part wishes
something will show up,
so someone will finally believe you.

MYALGIC ENCEPHALOMYELITIS (ME)

How am I to win
when it is ME
I am fighting against?

FADING FOOTSTEPS

I keep my feelings hidden behind stone
walls, showing just enough
to make you believe
I've said enough.

Sometimes tears would surface,
tongue tasting unspoken sorrow,
but only few, calculated words
escape through clenched teeth.

There is so much more
pushed deep below
every simple "I'm okay. Just tired"
or "I'll be fine. Just don't feel that well;"

so much more that I want
to express, but am scared to do so
for fear of hurting you more
than I have already.

I try to lower the gate
with those few words,
to let you know that I want to open up,
that I don't want to do this alone,

but you get upset
and I close up again,
hide my pain a little longer,
and finish crying after you leave,

whispering everything left unsaid
to your fading footsteps.

CLEANING A MIRROR AFTER AN IV TREATMENT

I wipe away the smudges
that wrinkle my face
and the dust that turns
my skin ashen—better,
but not quite
the healthy girl with the
persistent lively blush
I was hoping to see again.

Unable to clean
the dark grime collecting
in pockets under my eyes
or clear the fogginess
of the distant look within them,
I give up the ghost
of memory,
accepting this new visage.

There is still some grease
smearing my forehead
and fresh specks of rust
that dot bruised veins—
spots of green and blue
sprouting like mildew,
as though I am rotting
from the inside out.

PLEASE BE PATIENT

Please, be patient with me today.

I may not move as fast as you
would like,
my train of thought
seems to be experiencing some   delays,
and I may hesitate
before I speak,
trying to find the right words
that will most likely fumble
on my tongue
despite my effort.

Please, be patient with me today.

I am hurting
more than you know.

PAIN

Pain is a vine of thorns
with its source in the heart.

With each agonizing flare,
the vine grows—
a virus spreading
through the bloodstream—

thorns puncturing the walls
of the heart, tearing the lining
of the stomach, squeezing into the empty
space between cells.

You can hide the vine from prying
eyes, swallowing it like rancid medicine
that you believe you deserve, but you
can never rip the weed by its roots.

Eventually, with enough nourishment,
the vine will continue to expand
until the thorns have nowhere to go
but out. Piercing the flesh of your skin,

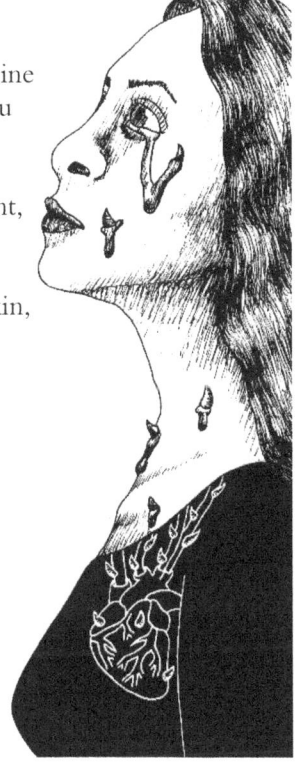

your pain protrudes—
exceeding its limits—your scars
become visible, and the secrets
you tried so hard to conceal

are exposed, bleeding
for all the world to see.

WAITING FOR THE PAIN TO PASS

I lie in silence, for the most part—
just the low murmur
of the TV downstairs,
the whispers of cars outside,
and a shuffle of distant
footsteps every now and then.

The dust settles around me
and I watch the colors
change on my ceiling—
first a sea of fire,
glowing embers in every
shade of amber,

then a pool of violet washes
across the canvas
as the night enters,
still and serene.
I like to think it is a secret
meant only for me.

WHEN SLEEP WON'T COME

Heart pounding
in the dark,
pulse thumping
in my ears,

mind racing
faster
than the cars
on the highway.

Perhaps sleep
won't come
until
peace does.

BRUISES WILL FADE

Bruises will fade,
but the memories will stain.

Wounds will heal,
but the scars will remain.

LIGHTNING STRIKES

I see her eyes
and know the storms had come,
raining steadily in the night.

I see her arms
and understand that lightning
never strikes the same place twice.

SAD STORIES

She so often consoled herself
with sad stories and tragic tales,
searching for a kindred fighter
to survive the misgivings bestowed by fate;
and when no hope was to be found,
she reminded herself
that it could always be worse.

WE ALL EXPERIENCE THE RAIN

We all experience
the rain differently.
For some, the droplets
collect in shallow
puddles, but for others,
they create an ocean
deep enough to drown.

STORMS AND RAINBOWS

Some days my mind swirls
in an unrelenting hurricane,
darkening the edges
where thoughts explode

in thunder and flash
by at lightning speed,
rain falling in torrents
that flood my view.

But I would rather have my mind
clouded by some rainy days
then suffer in the blinding
light of perpetual sunshine.

Because the storms
behind my eyes
reflect a vision of rainbows
when the sun shines again.

INTERLUDE: NATURE'S ELIXIR

ASH

Gazing out the window
to welcome the coming day

with pockets of mid-morning light
creating plush warmth
beneath my bare feet,

the torrid tingle of cinnamon tea
dancing on my tongue
like a crackling fire,

and dusty memories of yesterday
settling in the air,

glittering like ashes
in sunlight.

AMBER GLOW

I can stare for hours
at the amber glow
on the pine trees.

The light reminds me of the embers
within my heart, patiently waiting
for a spark to ignite.

ETERNAL DANCE

I've never been one to search
for rainbows,
though I will not deny their
evanescent beauty.

It is the intimate mingling of
light and shadow
that captivated my attention—

the gentle morning waltz
turned seductive tango
as the setting light flickers
to life with great urgency
that deepens the intentions
of her shadowy partners.

Light and shadow
sing to me their siren song,
for they mimic the
light and dark

within me, mingling
in an intimate dance
that took centuries to finesse.

FLOATING LEAVES

Leaves drop from the grand
oak trees above only to
get caught in the sky,

floating on the re-
flections of clouds as though they
never fell at all.

BIRD SONG

I ask the birds to sing
me a song,
and they always respond
with a sonnet.

IF MY HEART HAD WINGS

If my heart had wings,
where would it go?
Would it explore all the lands
I desire to know?

Would it fly with the birds
to places unseen,
to the places I long for
in each one of my dreams?

Or would it nestle in one place,
trading its wings for roots,
settling for the adventures
it can read about in books?

If my heart had wings,
where would it roam?
How far would it travel
to find somewhere to call home?

Would it flit from place to place,
searching for something grand,
finding home on the shores
of some distant land?

Or would it stop on a strange
shoulder along the way,
discover a kindred soul
and decide to stay?

Would it continue to soar,
or get tired and rest?
I guess I'll never know
with it caged in my chest.

SCENES FROM AN AIRPLANE WINDOW: 1

When the sun falls
beneath the ocean
of clouds,

the sky ignites
like a river
of molten lava.

COBBLESTONES

I would rather stumble
on ancient cobblestones
that line the streets of unfamiliar lands,
than glide with ease across
the same concrete sidewalks
that I walk every day.

PLACES REMEMBER

Sometimes places
remember *us*,
from a time lost
to the past, a time *we*
cannot remember,

and that pang
of familiarity is
the place whispering
to our soul,
"welcome home."

THE RED CITY

Desert-tainted fingers hold glaciers
in a cone. I taste the smooth
flavors of frozen flowers
upon my buds—
lavender,
rose,
violet—
as sticky lips attempt to pronounce
foreign streets where our footprints
overlap in trails of red dust,
indistinguishable.
Feet following the churches,
named after forgotten saints,
beacons for the wanderers
amongst the crowded buildings.

Roussillon, the red city,
erected upon rusted soil,
oxidized blood of the earth.
Like an oozing wound, seeping
into every crevice, from the seams
in warm flesh to the fissures
in graveyard bones—stitching
the city together with a single hue.

The sun-burnt ochre of the land
caked under our nails, inking
our cracked skin in intricate lacework
as we grasped more of the
rusty powder within our palms—
desert rouge smeared across
pristine pages, staining
our sketchbooks and our memories.

THE WATERS OF FONTAINE DE VAUCLUSE

Even the trees wanted
to share in the beauty,
arching their branches
to graze the surface
of the translucent waters.

FLUID TO FLESH

Well over fifty
percent water. Veins: currents
in a vast expanse.

The blood's mineral
composition reflects that
of the seven seas.

We're salty drops of
ocean wrapped in pliant flesh,
like water balloons.

Holding conch to ear,
blood sings to the tune of waves
crashing on the shore,

the soothing siren-
song of the ocean within
call us home again.

Our destiny is
not chiseled in heavy stone—
it's scribbled in salt

water that's written
in waving calligraphy
punctuated by

seafoam.

WITNESSING NATURE

Wisps of incense smoke
dance on the breeze,
trees grounded in the earth
yet, like me, reach for the sky,
ripples in the water
remind me that life is ever-flowing,
the light of the sun
glows amber on the world below,
and my spirit
bears witness to it all.

WOODS OF LEGEND: (A BROKEN TRAIL)

(Hiking from Bonnieux to Lacoste)

We walk a broken trail crowned in golden
leaves with velvety white bellies—
as though the painter

forgot to coat the underside—
that shimmer like stardust
as they rustle in the fading light.

The dusty lavender sky deepens
to a rich violet as we stride,
and the lights of the distant village

awaken for the night, twinkling
in the indigo hills like fallen stars.
Whipping dead leaves into a tunnel,

the wind bellows, calling my name,
and I suddenly know
how legends were born.

LESSONS FROM THE TREES:

I.

A mighty tree was once a seed
planted in total darkness
that persevered beyond
its limitation and surroundings.

You can either be swallowed
by the darkness
or sprout from it.

II.

Let the leaves fall as they may.
Discard the old skin
that no longer fits
to become the person
that you wish to be.
Shed and be reborn.

III.

Preserve your thick skin,
but always be a calm
and gentle presence,
providing comfort and shelter
for those in need
of a place to sit and an ear to listen.

IV.

Stay grounded,
rooted in reality,
but keep reaching skyward,
toward the dreams
awaiting you
on the clouds and stars.

V.

Any chance you get, take a moment
to stand completely still
and reflect on your surroundings.
Be at peace with where you are
and acknowledge that one day
this, too, may change.

VI.

Don't be afraid
to branch out
and try new things.
That is when the most growth occurs.

VII.

Stand tall and resolute,
being true to yourself and your beliefs,
but be open-minded enough
to allow yourself to be swayed
by the changing winds.

VIII.

Be strong but not too stubborn.
There will be many storms to weather,
and resilience comes from learning
how to bend without breaking.

IX.

Boughs break and leaves fall,
but that doesn't mean you are broken.

People will leave and you will lose
pieces of yourself
you believed to be permanent.
That is life. That is growth.

Perhaps they were never meant to last.
Let those pieces go and replace them with
something new,
something better,
something stronger.

THE IRONY OF TREES

Trees can live hundreds—
thousands—of years,
but never see the world
beyond their roots.
Yet they seem perfectly content
to call a single place home.

MAKE A WISH

Emerging from the woods
where we walked a broken
trail into the valley below,

we stumbled upon a patch
of dandelions with unruly
white tuffs ready to carry

our wishes to the stars.
We each picked one—
one dandelion, one wish—

a fair trade.
Like blowing out birthday candles,
my companions exhausted

the air in their lungs,
propelling their wishes
across the Luberon,

seeds taking flight
to sprout in distant lands.
It was my turn.

I gazed at the muddy tracks
leading to rustic houses,
acres of land turning

from green to goldenrod
before my eyes, grape vines
hanging in the mist,

and the smell of adventure
on the cool breeze.
I smiled.

It was the first time
I couldn't think of a wish,
for I was already living in a dream.

I MISS(ED) THIS

The sun's morning rays glint off the fountain's droplets
as they cascade into the rippling water, sparkling
like liquid diamonds, and illuminate
every shade of green in the surrounding foliage.

Oh, how I missed this…

The lush pine trees stand guard,
a protection from the oppressing world
heard rushing in the distance, with branches
reaching out to hold me in nature's embrace.

Oh, how I missed this…

The dewy autumn chill hanging
on the mid-morning breeze, sings on the skin
and whistles a fresh tune with each gust that rustles
the boughs of the pines and magnolia.

Oh, how I missed this…

The cardinals dance and croon with the wind
in a dazzle of rouge feathers, and the turtles
in the tranquil pond surface to breathe
the same crisp air that my lungs so easily welcome.

Oh, how I missed this…

The amber rays of the setting sun
reflecting off the pulsating water
in waves of undulating light
that set the trees ablaze.

Oh, how I missed this…

The simple peace that comes from sipping
a steaming cup of tea on a creaky wooden porch
in this serene oasis, where the only proof of time's existence
is in the falling leaves and slowly changing light.

Oh, how I will miss this.

SCENES FROM AN AIRPLANE WINDOW: II

Sailing across
a sea of cotton
over rivers of lights,

the world blanketed
by a quilt of stars,
a patchwork of constellations.

FREE BIRDS

But even free birds
need a place to rest
their wings.

FLORIDA SUMMER

Thick humidity fills the lungs,
like breathing wet cotton,
and takes form in the sweat
dripping off the brow.

Lizards scatter like cockroaches
across heated stones
to safety, and frogs croak
ominously from murky puddles
collecting under bushes.

Egrets scour the field for food
hidden beneath patches of brown
grass scorched by the sun.
Palm fronds droop low in the heat,

overlooking what used to be
swampland. Fossilized
coral and shells litter
the dirt, trying to remember
how the saltwater tasted.

COMPLIMENTS

Nature does not find
it's match or it's opposite.
Nature finds it's compliment,
just as the lush green branches
of the pine make their home
to the brilliant red cardinals.
And just like I found you.

ETERNAL CHASE

The Moon mourns the loss
that comes with the dawning
light of morning.

Her lover taken
from her soft embrace,
the blistering Sun

burning the Night away in a jealous rage.
The Day following in the Sun's wake,
envious of his fiery passion for another.

The Moon knew she could never love
the Sun when he steals all her light,
taking all she can give.

It is the Night that compliments
the Moon, letting his darkness
show so she can shine,

loving all her imperfections
that the Sun would hide
from view.

The Moon and the Night escape for a time
in each other's arms, before the Sun
chases them apart once more,

both longing
for an eternity
just out of reach.

LENDING ENERGY

The Sun has always
stolen my energy
while the Moon
gives me Hers.

THE DARKNESS, THE NIGHT, AND THE MOON

The darkness knows my secrets
and does not judge,

the night shows me who I am
without holding back,

and the moon teaches me to love myself
in a way that I never could.

AUTUMN CONTEMPLATIONS

Summer heat is trapped beneath the thicket
of green as the sun gets all the glory,
and winter sings the silent tune
that reveals the snow's chilling story.

Warm rain kisses the thirsty earth
when spring's flowers begin to bloom,
yet it is autumn's beauty that reminds us
of the journey's significance from womb to tomb.

In autumn, leaves bleed crimson
and the trees cry tears of gold,
as they shed their youthful skin, knowing
when it's time for another's tale to be told.

SNOW

The frozen shroud
that covers the earth in
white—the color of rebirth.

Winter ice
melts into
Spring's tears

as the gentle snow
buries the memories
of the past,

and gives birth
to the blossoming
year to come.

GEORGIA COLD

I sit on the porch
and stare at the newly
leafless trees,

letting the wintry cold
chill my skin to match
my numb heart.

STONES

You place stones above your
graven body—
the last marks you will
make in this world—
as evidence that you lived,
that you existed.

But, eventually, the carvings will fade
like the memory of you,
the stones will crumble
as they wither away to dust,
and your body, too,
will be reclaimed by the earth.

FALLEN LEAVES

The somber leaves lie
the morning after battle
like fallen soldiers.

WALKING IN THE RAIN

No one learned anything
from walking through shallow waters,
but I never thought I would drown
by getting caught in the rain.

(UPON) WAKING

I awaken to the sound of chirping birds,
starry sleep still trapped in my lungs,
and a soft purring in my ear.

The remnants of dreams
on my eyelashes burn to dust
with the first rays of the sun,

and morning flowers
carry the teardrops
of the mourning moon.

RELAPSE

A STOLEN KISS

Sunshine warms my skin
with a gentle touch that leaves
a tingling on my lips,
then vanishes just as quickly
as dark clouds consume the light
and rain begins to fall,
like a stolen kiss,
lingering only in memory.

RELAPSE

There is a difference
between falling in reverse
and falling forward.

There is a difference
between falling back down to stand before
the mountain you already climbed,

and falling forward
down the mountain
to stand before a new one.

When you fall forward,
you will be left
scraped and bruised and scarred,

just as if you had fallen
in the opposite direction,
but you will still be moving ahead,

confronting a new challenge,
more difficult than the last,
but one that will take you to new heights.

When you rise, you could be deep
in the valley you hoped to avoid,
but you will still be farther along

than you were before,
and what made you tumble
will be a thing of the past.

But when you fall in reverse,
you are regressing, moving backward
along the path you once traveled,

and if you manage to rise to your feet,
you will eventually stand
in the same place,

facing the same obstacle
that pushed you over the edge,
with the threat of falling once more.

GHOST

What to do when you realize
that you are the ghost
of your former self—

forced to occupy
your new life,
destined to repeat
your past mistakes?

MAY NEVER GET BETTER

Will you stay with me
until I get better?
And will you still love me
knowing that I may never?

DECEMBER NIGHTS

The tree's twinkling lights flicker
in my eyes, giving a sense of liveliness
to the cold, dull
brown—the color
of grave dirt.

A mixture of eggnog and spirits
dampens the pain, bringing
a smile and a rosy blush
to my pale cheeks
that could rival Santa's.

Laughter escapes like the bubbles
in my drink, and champagne-
stained breath sweetens the carols
I sing, masking my illness
from people who do not wish to see it.

LISTEN

I find it ironic how the people
I want to listen, seem to pull away
when I need a place to lean.

And the ones who do, listen
closely, intently looking
for a secret to hold

against me, or a way to twist
my words into balloon animals
so that I appear a clown.

But in the moment, they seem so kind,
so willing to help, and I yearn
to be understood.

So I mistakenly trust them as they smile
sweetly, internally mapping the streams
of tears, so they can find them again.

A CONVERSATION

"Why didn't you tell me
it was this bad?"

> *"You told me long ago*
> *to not tell you anything...*
> *so you wouldn't get upset."*

"Oh, so its been going on
for that long then, huh?"

> *"It has never stopped."*

MY LIGHT

"She is my light,"
you say, pausing,
not bothering
to state what *I* am to you,
but implying it, nonetheless.

For if she is your light—
your savior, like her namesake—
then I must surely be
your darkness, the despair
from which you seek refuge.

"She is my light,"
you repeat,
this time continuing,
"and *I* am trying
to be *your* light."

What I thought
and should have said:

*I don't need a light—
I am my own light,
and my future is my hope—
but it would be nice
to have a hand
to help steady me
once in a while
when my world shakes.*

CARBON

When I was younger,
I used to believe
she was indestructible,
and I wanted to be
just as formidable.

But as I grew older
and more ill
I realized that I was always
the strong one, and she
threatens to come apart

at the seams
with a single whisper.
If we were both made
of carbon,
then she is the pencil's graphite—

sharpened for show,
but breaks under the pressure—
and I am the diamond—
rough and raw—but able
to withstand the heat.

EGGSHELLS

I sit,
picking eggshells
from my calloused feet
after a conversation
with you.

SUFFOCATING

Putting a timestamp
on my health
is suffocating,
like a plastic bag
being forced over my head,
preventing fresh air
from filling my lungs
as I writhe and clutch
at my aching throat.
It gives (false) hope,
to me and to you,
and will make me feel
like a failure
if my body is unable
to meet your deadline.

"PLEASE RATE YOUR PAIN AND FATIGUE

on a scale from one to ten,
ten being the worst."

I always struggle with this

because to answer correctly,
I need to remember
what it felt like
to be well,
and I've given up hoping
for a one through five
long ago.

So I mistook
a nine for a seven
just because it wasn't a ten
that day.

AFTER YEARS

After years of pain,
what does "better" feel like?
Having grown accustomed
to the daily agony,
the daily struggle,
I barely remember
what it was like before.
And I'm not sure
I want to know
what it's like again,
because I don't know
if I'll be able to bear
the pain should it return.

NEVER IS A PAINFUL WORD

It is not the loneliness that hurts—
I enjoy being alone.
It is all the smiles
I never wore,
all the regrets
for risks never taken,
all the experiences
I never shared,
and all the stories
I will never get to tell.

NO KISS ON NEW YEAR'S

"Your New Year's kiss
is out there waiting for you."

Or maybe he isn't waiting,
but loving a mistake instead,
unaware of my existence
as I count another
year gone and he counts
the seconds till he gets to touch her
lips with his.

NEVER WAS

Oh, how I long for the day
when these poems
are of heartbreak and love lost
than love that never was.

(UN)CHECKED BOXES

I.

My days are consumed
by the tedious tasks
on my regular to do lists.

No mention of health
or happiness—there is no
time, no room between

the consuming responsibilities
doled out by others
that always take higher priority.

I check off one, and three
fill its place,
like a hydra

only the strongest could slay.
But my strength wanes
and I am no hero.

Unfinished tasks are
added to the next day
and the day after that—

days blur together
as yesterday's incompletions
become today's burdens,

and pen scratches paper
like the continuous
ticking of a clock—

Tick, check.
Tick, check.
Tick, check.

II.

There is a list
etched on the chambers
of my heart.

A special list of wishes
and dreams and desires
that defines my life
and everything I hope
it to be.

It is very short,
very simple,
no boxes checked.

My life is a series of
unchecked boxes.
Things I have not done,
and things I have yet to experience,

What if all that is left
of me one day
is a pile of unchecked boxes?
My life defined by
the things I was never able to do.

SAME PERSON

She proudly states that she is the same
person as she was thirty years ago—as
though that is something to be admired,
something everyone should strive to achieve.

But I will proudly admit that I am not the same
person as I was a year ago, let alone decades ago.
And I do not want to be the same
person in one year, two years, or thirty years.

I want to change. I want to evolve. I want to grow.
And I hope that years from now, or even tomorrow,
I am a healthier, smarter, braver, kinder, stronger, wiser,
better
person than I am today.

IN THE EFFORT OF PROGRESS

In my mind,
I have climbed mountains,
crossed deserts,
and sailed over seas.

But to the world,
others have run miles,
while I have barely
moved an inch.

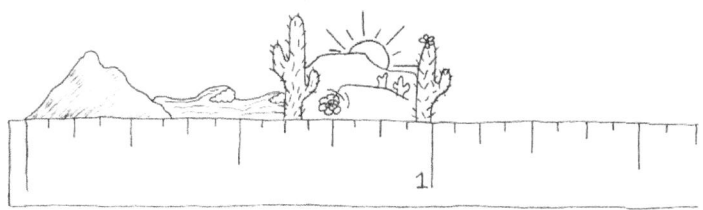

LOVELY DREAM

Is it possible to have known
someone before the scars?

If so, was it really them,
or just a lovely dream?

NO PLACE TO HIDE: II

I wonder if people fear the dark
because they fear the parts of themselves
that they try to lock away,
and in the dark, there is no place to hide.

FRAIL

Despite my height,
large bones,
and inner lioness,

when my illness comes
like the changing tides
and crashes like a tsunami,

I fear that I may
fall apart and float away
like a dandelion in the breeze.

ANCHORS

I am so close to the surface,
light scattering in a beckoning call,
and know that there is fresh,
satisfying air just beyond.

I reach upward, fighting against
the chains digging angrily into my flesh,
trying to drag me down
into the shadowy depths.

I've endured these anchors
for so long already, battling bravely,
but I don't know how much longer
I can hold my breath.

I'M TIRED OF BEING TIRED—

of waking after over twelve hours of deep slumber
as though I had not slept at all;
of fatigued limbs that don't move as I wish,
though my mind begs them to keep going;
of my young joints screaming in protest
like the creaky floorboards of an old house.

I'm tired of doctors' appointments
that lead to nowhere
except prescriptions and pill bottles;
of IVs threaded through my veins
and the needlepoint scars
trailing up my arms like ant bites.

I'm tired of bruised eyes staring
back from the mirror,
the purple flesh evidence
of my body's constant fight,
and how I notice a little less liveliness
swimming in my irises
than the day before.

I'm tired of having to explain myself,
of the looks people give
when they don't understand,
and their lack of attempt at trying.

I'm tired of a life filled with compromises;
of having a wild soul trapped
in a body that can't sustain it.

I'm so tired of being tired.

A TOAST TO MY FORMER SELF (WHEREVER YOU MAY BE)

Here's to the girl
I never got to know,
the girl that I lost
a long time ago.

I hope that her life
has been filled with ease,
reaching with strong
hands for every possibility—

traveling to all the places
she desired to see,
to the places I can only explore
inside of my dreams.

Having never experienced
those stolen years,
she propelled forward
without any fears.

No tears had stained
her wild eyes,
and through her smiling
lips passed no lies.

It may have a few scratches,
but her heart is still whole,
and she never questions
the voice guiding her wandering soul.

I hope that her life is painless,
everything she wished it to be,
and that she is viewing the world
somewhere as a better version of me.

MY PROMISE TO YOU

I will lead you through
the dark labyrinth,
for I once walked
it, too.

Follow my lead,
accept your power,
and you will be born
anew.

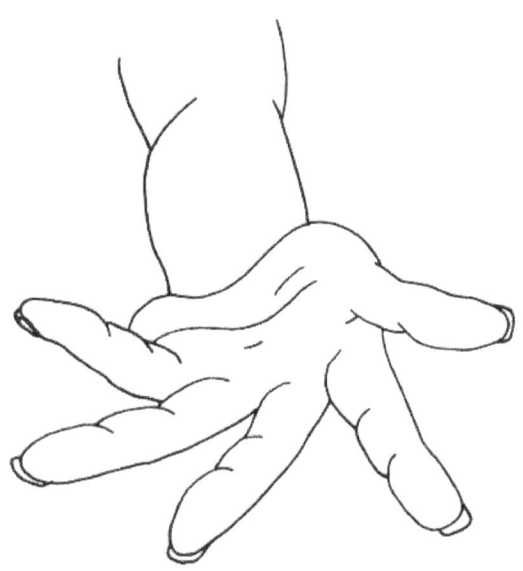

RESILIENCE

A LESSON FROM PERSEPHONE

Scratching, clawing,
fighting to break free—
that was how
Persephone entered the Underworld,
a place not meant for her young and vibrant nature.

Desperate, trapped,
caged and gasping for air—
that was how
Persephone felt when captured,
forced into a life not of her choosing.

But she was no fragile bird,
she was a budding goddess.
She could not alter her situation,
so she changed the one thing she could:
herself.

The goddess of Spring and Rebirth
did just that—
transformed through death.
She laid her past to rest,
blossoming into a force all her own.

Rather than wallowing,
she gained control,
turning imprisonment into opportunity,
and made herself a queen—

Queen of the Damned,
but a queen nonetheless,
with all the power
and glory that entails.

EMBRACE THE DARKNESS

Embrace the darkness.
Make peace with your demons
and shadows, the ghosts
still haunting you.

The light will shine,
the sun will rise in the morning
and taste just as sweet
upon the skin as in memory.

But when the night descends again,
you can be sure that there will be
nothing to fear—for you will have become
the most fearsome of creatures within its depths.

READING BETWEEN THE LINES

Reading gives me solace—
to be able to leap
into another world,
if only for a short while.

But as much as I yearn
to crawl between the lines
on the dusty pages
and call them home,

the story is not mine,
the life is not mine,
and I refuse to be written
as a supporting character.

ARROW

How lovely it would seem to be the sword:
sharp, intimidating—a mighty force
that few obstacles could avert.

Yet I appear to be the arrow:
pulled back—further and further
away from its target with each passing moment.

But that is okay for now. I will not be deterred.
Because I know that the further I am pulled
back—the tighter the tension builds—the farther
I will soar when the time comes   to   fly.

GLUED TOGETHER

Let the tears fall.

Let the streaming droplets
fill the cracks
and line the jagged edges,
gluing your broken pieces
back together.

No, you will never be
as you once were,
but you will be whole
once again.

THE GIRL IN THE MIRROR

What I tell the girl in the mirror,
chanting in time to the battle drum
that pulses in my ears with each heartbeat:

Your red-rimmed eyes and dark circles are battle paint—
red and black, fire and ash.

Your bruises are badges of honor—
reminders that you are fighting unseen enemies daily,

that sitting motionless with an IV in your arm
is a courageous leap forward.

Your tears are not weakness,
they are a source of healing

and will eventually cleanse your body,
washing away all your pain.

You may have lost the battle,
but you *will* win the war.

You are not falling apart,
you are falling together.

HOPE, RESURRECTED

Hope is all that remains
after the doctor told me
there is no cure.
That hope may be a fish
out of water, starving for attention
and flipping about as it begs to breathe again.
That hope may die
and wither away to dried bones,
but its carcass will remain, waiting
for its impending resurrection, like Lazarus.

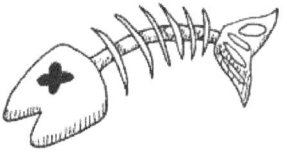

HAIKU OF HOPE

Hope is the seedling
burrowed in broken hearts that
blooms when sadness smiles.

CRY, IF YOU WANT

Cry, if you want,
feel what you need
to feel—sadness,
anger, frustration—
let it all out.

You don't need to
always be happy,
but you do need
to be positive—

you have every right
to be sad, to feel
the way you do, but you need
to believe that there are
better days ahead.

Cry, if you want,
let out all the pain,
but be sure not to
drown in your sorrows.

So if you must cry, grow
from your tears,
and bloom like a flower
after the rain.

NEVER FORGET

Never forget how they
made you feel,
no matter how much
you love and forgive them.

Keep in mind that "sorry"
is not in their vocabulary
and they will never
learn its true meaning.

Never forget that you
would give them hours
and they wouldn't spare
a minute,

that you are just
a disappointment
they like to remind
you of.

Never forget that they
are just waiting to make you cry,
or that they will try to crush your
hopes when given the chance,

no matter how much
you want to and would do
anything to see a smile
brighten their face.

Never forget that they
tried to cripple you
with words when you
were already down

for the count,
taking the first opportunity
to diminish and disrespect you
when you weren't looking.

Never forget how their
eyes shine like jewels
when they see you crawling
to make amends,

trying to be a better person
when you are on your hands and knees
because you would rather apologize
for doing nothing than to live without them.

Never forget that they
tried to hurt you when it was convenient
for them, or that they sharpened
their tongue to watch you bleed,

and how their smile is a promise
that they will do it all again
and again
and again.

CAGED TIGERS

I've been pushed back,
back against the bars
that dare to hold me captive,
but I refuse to be made a victim—

I have earned my stripes
and will put them to use,
my claws sharpened,
ready to attack.

Caged tigers are the most
dangerous of creatures
because they have
nothing left to lose.

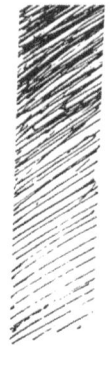

INTENSITY

I put up walls
to contain the power
that surges through my veins.

But I learned that
I cannot grow stronger
until these dams burst.

I should not apologize
for this intensity, for nature does not
apologize for Her storms.

THE FIERY CROWN

My hair is a battle cry,
the declaration that sparked
an unseen war, a warning
to those who would dare
to mess with me—

think again.
The blood-stained coils
lapping against my pale,
bruised skin and sleepless
eyes in a fiery crown,

are proof that I have not
been scorched by hellfire,
but have absorbed the inferno,
becoming more powerful
than I could ever imagine.

And should I burn,
I will rise from the ashes
even stronger, for
I have tasted the flames
and will not surrender
without blood and fire.

LIKE THE SUN

(for my sister)

You are like the sun,
shining so brightly,
you ignite the dark;

but, like the sun,
you are blinded
to your own light.

MONUMENTAL

They do not understand me,
for I am not made of clay.
They cannot mold me,
shape me into a form they desire
that is not of my choosing.

I am stone, chiseled
by my own hands.
My presence scares
them because chipped stone
is not as easily fixed as cracked clay.

I am a monument, a lasting reminder
that I do not surrender easily.
I may be worn down
by the storms I've weathered,
but I am still just as strong as before.

STONE WINGS

These stone wings weren't meant to fly,
but they are strong and will lift me to greater heights
than delicate feathers ever could.

THE PATH THEY PAVED

Thank you to the women
who blazed the trail
before me,
scorching the ground
beneath their bare,
calloused feet.

I will not let you down.

May I travel further
along the path
they paved,
illuminating the course
for others to follow,
like the way they guided me.

I will not let your fight be in vain.

I, TOO, SHALL DIG

(Homage to the poem Digging *by Seamus Heaney)*

With this pen and with this ink,

I will dig, ploughing fields for those in need of nourishment,

I will dig gardens to plant seeds of hope,

I will dig wells to quench thirst and to safeguard wishes,

I will dig trenches for the battles worth fighting,

I will dig graves to bury the pain and sorrow of the past,

I will dig burrows for wary heads to rest,

I will dig for the hidden treasure in every soul,

I will dig, mining for dreams amongst the darkness.

With this pen and with this heart,
I, too, shall dig.

ROADMAP

"Don't dwell on the past,"
he says.

"It isn't dwelling,"
I say.
"It's reflecting."

Look to the future,
but remember the past,
for it is a roadmap
of experience.

If you don't check the map
every now and then,
you may lose direction—perhaps
take a wrong turn—

and instead of moving forward,
toward where you are
meant to be, you may end
up where you've already been.

THE ROAD TO RECOVERY

You would think by now
it would be a highway—
straight and direct—considering
the amount of people
that have traversed this path.

Yet the road enjoys
the scenic route,
with its twists and unexpected
turns, mostly uphill.
But I hear that the view at the end is incredible.

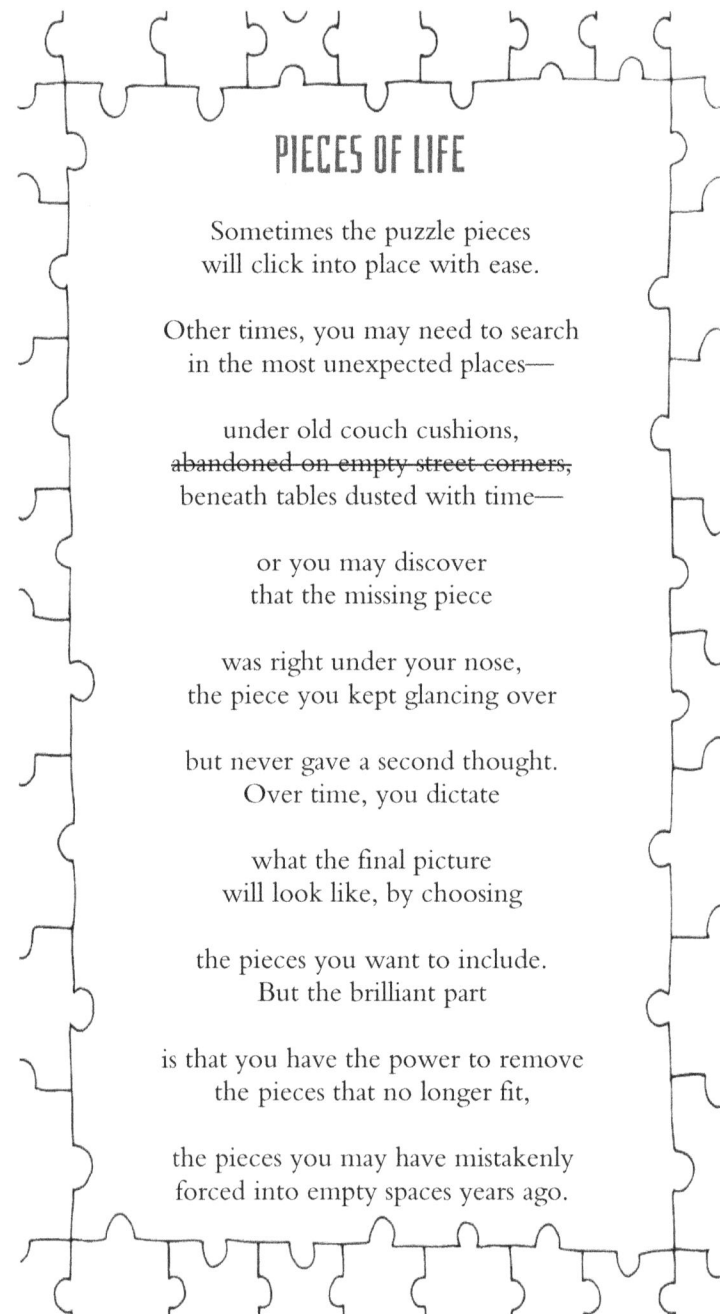

PIECES OF LIFE

Sometimes the puzzle pieces
will click into place with ease.

Other times, you may need to search
in the most unexpected places—

under old couch cushions,
~~abandoned on empty street corners,~~
beneath tables dusted with time—

or you may discover
that the missing piece

was right under your nose,
the piece you kept glancing over

but never gave a second thought.
Over time, you dictate

what the final picture
will look like, by choosing

the pieces you want to include.
But the brilliant part

is that you have the power to remove
the pieces that no longer fit,

the pieces you may have mistakenly
forced into empty spaces years ago.

EQUATING FREEDOM

I find that most people equate
freedom with flight,
flying as a means to escape
their earthly limitations.
For they feel that they can only
be truly free if they keep flitting
from place to place,
afraid to land
and risk growing roots.
But what does the sky
have to offer
aside from a better view
of all that you once had?

FREEDOM

Freedom is not simply
being able to leave,
but also having
the choice to stay.

EXQUISITE SOULS

We are told to hide
our scars, tears, blemishes—
any noticeable and undesirable
imperfections.

But I wonder if the people
who want us to mask ourselves,
could show me an exquisite soul
that isn't flawed.

YOU ARE NOT ALONE.

There are plenty of broken
people, healing
at their own pace.

The world
is stitched together
with scars.

WRITE MYSELF WHOLE

I write to heal myself,
and I intend to write
myself whole,

stitching myself together
one word at
a time.

THANK YOU

I would like to thank
the illness that

broke me,
shattered me,

disintegrated me.
It is from those ashes

that I was able to rebuild
myself and establish a stronger

person from the debris.
You set out to annihilate me,

but have instead
created anew.

You are the source
of both my destruction

and my strength,
finding my weaknesses

and pressing me to improve
upon them.

This beautiful, powerful
creature would not have existed

if it were not for the wreckage
you caused.

You hurt me, as you always do,
but I have vowed to never allow

you to harm me
in the same way.

I have become a hydra,
learning from your actions—

the more you maim me,
the more resilient I become,

the more pieces you take away,
the more I will grow back,

filling the empty spaces
with armor.

If you cripple me,
I will sprout wings.

If you cut me down,
I will grow a forest.

If you feed me to the wolves,
I will sharpen my teeth to match their fangs.

If you burn me,
I will rise like a phoenix.

If you force me to crack under the pressure,
you will find a diamond underneath.

And if you push me to supernova,
I will create a whole universe.

You will continue to torment me
as you course through my veins,

and I have accepted that fate.
But I refuse to accept defeat.

ON ANOTHER NOTE...

To my illness:

> Thank you
> for all that you've taken,
> for all that you've given.
>
> Now fuck off!

ACKNOWLEDGEMENTS

With greatest thanks to:

My family, for your constant love and support. My mom and dad—Tracey and Scott—for helping me find my wings and giving me a place to land. My sister, Sabrina, for being the sunshine of our family, bringing much love and light into my life, and for always knowing how to make me laugh. Additional thanks to my mom and sister for being my unofficial editors.

Honey Bun and Binx, the sweetest fur-babies, for your unconditional love, emotional support, and healing kisses.

Dana and Kacie, for showing me the true meaning of friendship.

The entire Atmosphere team, for seeing potential in my words and helping to make my dream a reality.

The doctors who refused to give up on me, for providing hope and a fighting chance.

My autoimmune condition, for teaching me pain, patience, and perseverance. I wouldn't be the person I am today without you.

You, dearest reader, for picking up this book and joining me on this journey. Thank you for having the courage to fight your daily battles, even when they go unrecognized. I understand the pain and I see you. You are so much stronger than you realize, and you continue to inspire me every day.

ABOUT ATMOSPHERE PRESS

Atmosphere Press is an independent, full-service publisher for excellent books in all genres and for all audiences. Learn more about what we do at atmospherepress.com.

We encourage you to check out some of Atmosphere's latest releases, which are available at Amazon.com and via order from your local bookstore:

The Unsolvable Intrigue, poetry by D.C. Stoy

Words of a Feather Hawked Together, poetry by Linda Marie Hilton

I Am Not Young And I Will Die With This Car In My Garage, poetry by Blake Z. Rong

Love, Air, poetry by Lawdenmarc Decamora

To Let Myself Go, poetry by Kimberly Olivera Lainez

less on that later, poetry by Madeline Farber

The Last Hello: 99 Odes to the Body, poetry by Joe Numbers

Granddaughter of Dust, poetry by Laura Williams

Nest of Stars, poetry by Nicole Verrone

Damaged, poetry by Crystal Wells

I Would Tell You a Secret, poetry by Hayden Dansky

Aegis of Waves, poetry by Elder Gideon

Footnotes for a New Universe, by Richard A. Jones

Streetscapes, poetry by Martin Jon Porter

Feast, poetry by Alexandra Antonopoulos

River, Run! poetry by Caitlin Jackson

Poems for the Asylum, poetry by Daniel J. Lutz

Licorice, poetry by Liz Bruno

ABOUT THE AUTHOR

Jennifer Sara Widelitz graduated with a BFA in Visual Effects from the Savannah College of Art and Design and worked as a compositor, creating special effects for film and television. She is an artist with a deep-rooted passion for storytelling in a variety of mediums: film, photography, writing, painting, poetry, etc. She likes to view the world as a grand storybook and can't wait to see what adventures the next chapter brings. This is her first poetry collection, although her poetry and photography have appeared in several literary publications. Much of her poetry is based in her personal experience with autoimmunity and chronic invisible illness, writing for the rebels and warriors, the survivors of the human condition who fight all kinds of unseen battles. She is a dog lover and a cat mommy, and is rarely seen without a cup of tea or a good book.

To find out more, visit
https://jenniferwidelitz.com/ or follow her on:

Instagram:
@jennifersarawidelitz (personal)
or @jswpoetry (poetry)

Twitter:
@jswidelitz

Made in the USA
Monee, IL
20 April 2022

95087545R00100